I Smiled Today

A Book on Mourning and Healing

Pamela Govender

A catalogue record for this book is available from the National Library of Australia

Copyright © 2024 Pamela Govender
All rights reserved.
ISBN-13: 978-1-923174-04-7

Linellen Press
265 Boomerang Road
Oldbury, Western Australia
www.linellenpress.com.au

In Loving Memory

In Loving Memory of my late Mum, late Dad and my dear brother, Rodney Naidoo, my cousins Christopher Maistry and Wesley Maistry and my uncles Roy Samuel and Jaya Samuel.

In Loving Memory is not just a dedication; it's a pledge to celebrate the lives that once graced our days and touched our hearts. It is an acknowledgment that their memory lives on in the love we carry, in the wisdom we inherit and in grace we find healing. It is a tribute to the enduring impact of their presence, forever etched in the story of our lives.

Acknowledgements

I want to express my deep appreciation to my husband, Seelan, and sons, Kaylan and Nikiel, for being my steadfast pillars of strength during my time of loss. Your unwavering support, endless patience, and boundless encouragement laid the necessary foundation for this endeavour. This book stands as a testament to the love and support I've found within our home. You've not just been my family but also my partners in navigating the complexities of grief. Your presence and understanding have been the guiding lights that fuelled the creation of this work.

With heartfelt gratitude for the unity and love that defines our family.

Contents

I changed my address today 1
    Verse 3
    Word of encouragement: 4
    Prayer 5
    Daily Journal 6

In your memory, I carry on 9
    Verse 10
    Word of encouragement: 11
    Prayer 12
    Daily Journal 13

Nothing prepares you for all the firsts 15
    Verse 16
    Word of encouragement: 17
    Prayer 18
    Daily Journal 19

In his presence, my resting place 21
    Verse 22
    Word of encouragement: 23
    Prayer 24
    Daily Journal 26

I smiled today	*29*
Verse	*31*
Word of encouragement:	*32*
Prayer	*33*
Daily Journal	*34*
Removing the mask	*36*
Verse	*38*
Word of encouragement:	*39*
Prayer	*40*
Daily Journal	*41*
The language of tears	*43*
Verse	*45*
Word of encouragement:	*46*
Prayer	*47*
Daily Journal	*48*
My mirror	*51*
Verse	*52*
Word of encouragement:	*53*
Prayer	*54*
Daily Journal	*55*

A piece of me 57
    Verse 59
    Word of encouragement: 60
    Prayer 62
    Daily Journal 63

A promise I'll keep… 65
    Verse 66
    Word of encouragement: 67
    Prayer 68
    Daily Journal 69

In the stillness of 2am 71
    Verse 72
    Word of Encouragement: 73
    Prayer 74
    Daily Journal 75

Lonely, but not alone 77
    Verse 78
    Word of Encouragement: 79
    Prayer 80
    Daily Journal 81

Beyond the Door 83
    Verse 84
    Word of Encouragement: 85
    Prayer 86
    Daily Journal 87

Shadows in our home 89
    Verse 90
    Word of Encouragement 91
    Prayer 92
    Daily Journal 93

Why me? 95
    Verse 96
    Word of Encouragement: 97
    Prayer 98
    Daily Journal 99

An everyday prayer for mourning and grieving 100

Prayer for myself 102

Daily Journal *104*

Daily Journal *105*

Daily Journal *106*

Daily Journal *107*

Daily Journal *108*

Daily Journal *109*

Daily Journal *110*

Daily Journal *111*

I changed my address today

Sorry we didn't get a chance to say goodbye,
A gentle voice was calling me.
Earthly trials and tears no more,
peace and joy forevermore.

So, smile and wipe away the tears,
I ain't that far away,
Don't think of me as gone forever,
I only changed my address today.

I changed my address today;
God called me home.
I changed my address today;
Heaven is now my home.

I changed my address today,
Heaven is a promised dream.
He has given me better
than the best I've ever dreamed.

I changed my address today,
I know you are asking God Why?
You see, I have finished my race,
We are all running at a different pace.

I changed my address today,
I have entered heaven's gates.
His promises are real …
he surely has prepared a place.

I changed my address today,
and I am not home alone,
it was the biggest family reunion
I have ever known.

I changed my address today,
I am home sweet home.
In a place that's filled with joy
and everlasting love – safe now up above.

I changed my address today,
Heaven is for real; just you wait and see.
I changed my address today,
And the Lord face to face I see.

On that joyous day when God calls you home,
I will meet you at heaven's gate,
In the meantime, smile, love and go on.
I only changed my address today.

See you later!

Verse

John 14:2-3: "My Father's house has many rooms; if that were not so, would I have told you that I am going there to prepare a place for you? And if I go and prepare a place for you, I will come back and take you to be with me that you also may be where I am."

This verse summarises the message that Jesus is conveying to his disciples. In this verse, he assures them that in his Father's house, there are many dwelling places and that he is going to prepare a place for them. He promises to return and take them with him so that they can be together in the place he has prepared. This verse expresses Jesus' promise of an eternal home in heaven for his followers, where they will be reunited with him. It offers hope and assurance of a future with Christ.

Word of encouragement:

In times of grief, mourning and a broken heart, this verse offers profound hope and assurance. It reminds us that our earthly life is not the end of the story, but rather the beginning of a journey leading to a beautiful reunion in the presence of God.

Take solace in the belief that, in God's plan, there is a place prepared for your loved one in his heavenly house. The pain of separation is temporary and, one day, there will be a joyful and eternal reunion with them. In that place, there will be no more pain, sorrow, or separation.

In the midst of your grief and broken heart, know that God's love and promises are unwavering. He is preparing a place for you and your loved ones, and the tears of this world will be replaced by the joy of eternity. The night of weeping will give way to a morning of rejoicing in his presence.

Your faith is a source of strength and God's love is a constant and enduring presence in your life. Lean on your faith, for you are not alone in your grief. God is with you, guiding you through the darkness of sorrow and into the eternal light of his love. This promise in John 14:2-3 is a testament to the everlasting nature of God's love and the hope of a beautiful reunion in his presence.

Prayer

Our Dear Heavenly Father, as I go through these days of mourning and grief, I come before you with a heavy heart.

I seek your comfort, your solace, and your peace, Lord. Your promise in John 14:2-3 brings me hope, reminding me that there is a place prepared in your heavenly home for my loved one.

I thank you for the assurance that we will be reunited in your presence, free from pain and sorrow. Though we are separated for a time, I know that we will share a glorious dwelling place in your eternal kingdom.

Lord, during these moments of grief, help me find strength in your love. Bring me the peace that surpasses all understanding. May I remember your promise and find comfort in it. I trust that you have welcomed my loved one into your arms and I am grateful for the joy and everlasting love they now experience.

Guide me through the process of healing, Lord. May your presence be a constant source of support and may I be encouraged to smile and love in the midst of my sorrow.

Help me trust completely in the promises you've made and may I look forward to the day of our joyful reunion.

I am grateful for the hope, comfort, and assurance you provide. In this time of mourning, I find strength in your words and promises. Be with me, Lord, as I continue this journey of grief and help me keep the faith that leads to eternal joy and reunion.

In Jesus' precious name, I pray, Amen.

Daily Journal

In your memory, I carry on

In your memory, I carry on, though this pain feels so strong.
In your memory, I carry on, honouring you from dusk till dawn.

The battles you faced with unwavering grace,
And through the challenges of life, you found your place.
Leaving a legacy of kindness and a warm embrace.

In the quiet of night, your presence feels near,
Memories of your laughter bring solace and cheer.
Through each new chapter, as I journey along,
In your memory, I will find the strength to be strong.

In my heart, you're alive, and I'll carry you.
In my thoughts, my actions, I'll remember you too.
Though your voice may be no more, your words still remain.
In the quietest moments, they soothe my pain.

In the chapters I write, in the roles I portray,
With your memory alive in me, I will treasure each passing day.
In my heart, you will forever live on,
In my memory, you are never gone.

So, I journey onward through each new day,
I will always remember you in a very special way.

Verse

Psalm 34:18: "The Lord is close to the broken-hearted and saves those who are crushed in spirit."

This verse reminds us that, in times of deep emotional pain and when our spirits are crushed, God is not far away. He is intimately involved in our suffering, offering his presence and the saving grace needed to heal our broken hearts and restore our crushed spirits. It's a message of reassurance, highlighting God's compassion and care for those who are going through difficult moments.

Word of encouragement:

In times of grief and mourning, it's essential to remember that you are not alone in your pain. God is near and his compassionate presence is a source of comfort and strength. He understands the depth of your sorrow and the weight on your spirit.

Take solace in the knowledge that God is a healer and a restorer of the broken-hearted. While the pain of loss may seem overwhelming, there is hope for healing and renewal. Lean on your faith and trust that God's love is constant and unchanging, even in the midst of profound sorrow.

It's okay to grieve and mourn, as it is a natural and necessary part of the healing process. Know that you can bring your broken heart and crushed spirit to God in prayer. Pour out your sorrows before him and allow his love and grace to bring you comfort and restoration.

Remember that eventually, the night of weeping will give way to the morning of rejoicing. Your grief will not last forever and God will guide you through it. You are loved and, in your brokenness, you can find strength and hope in the loving embrace of the Lord.

Prayer

Our Dear Heavenly Father, in the midst of my sorrow and brokenness, I turn to you, the source of comfort and strength. I find solace in the words of Psalm 34:18, which reminds me that you are near to me in my pain and aware of my suffering.

Lord, I need your divine intervention in my life. I thank you for your promise of salvation, healing and comfort as I am overwhelmed by grief and sorrow. I acknowledge that even in my deepest despair, there is hope in you and that you are the source of my spiritual restoration when I feel crushed.

Today, I lift up my heavy heart to you. Please comfort me and grant me the peace that surpasses all understanding. Bring healing, Lord, and give me the strength to face the days ahead.

Help me feel your presence and guidance in the midst of my grief. Let me know that I am not alone. Grant me the assurance that, through your grace, I can find renewal and hope, even during profound sorrow.

I pray for the wisdom to understand that grief is a process, and I trust in your perfect timing for healing. Give me the patience and strength I need as I go through this challenging journey.

I surrender this heavy burden to you, Lord. I know that you are my source of comfort and peace. Guide me out of the darkness of grief and may your presence be a source of strength and restoration.

In Jesus' precious name, I pray. Amen.

Daily Journal

Nothing prepares you for all the firsts

Nothing prepares you for all the firsts,
The journey is hard, and it only gets worse.
The first time I heard your favourite song,
It played in my head all day long.
In that moment the song brought you near,
In the lyrics, I still hold you very dear.

My first Christmas without you, it is so hard to bear,
In my heart, you're a gift beyond compare.
A bond unbroken, a love always there.
The first birthday without you,
I will no doubt shed a tear,
But I must cherish the moments when you were here.

For the first time when I visit your resting place,
With flowers and a heavy heart,
I will remember your love and your warm embrace.

For the firsts will always bring pain,
That much is true,
But I know with God's grace,
I'll find the strength to see it through.

Verse

Psalm 30:5: "For his anger lasts only a moment, but his favour lasts a lifetime; weeping may stay for the night, but rejoicing comes in the morning."

This verse offers a message of comfort, reminding us that difficult times, sorrows, and hardships are temporary. God's favour and joy are lasting and after a night of weeping and sorrow, there is the promise of a morning filled with rejoicing and happiness. It encourages us to persevere through challenges, knowing that brighter days will follow and God's enduring love and blessings are always present.

Word of encouragement:

In the midst of mourning and a heavy heart, it's natural to feel the weight of grief and loss. The night of weeping may seem long and dark, but the promise of this verse reminds us that joy will come in the morning. Just as the dawn follows the darkest hour of the night, so too will your sorrow eventually give way to moments of rejoicing.

God's love and favour are steadfast and everlasting. Even when we face moments of sorrow and pain, his grace remains constant. It's okay to grieve and it's okay to weep, for these are natural and necessary parts of the healing process.

In your time of mourning, remember that God is near and his love is enduring. You are not alone in your grief. Lean on your faith and trust that with his grace you will find the strength to endure. The night of weeping may be long, but it will not last forever. Your heavy heart will gradually find relief and you will discover moments of joy and light once more.

Prayer

Our Dear Heavenly Father, today I come before you in the mighty name of Jesus. I turn to you, my source of hope and comfort. Your Word in Psalm 30:5 reminds me that, while we may endure moments of weeping, joy will come in the morning and your favour lasts a lifetime.

Lord, I feel the weight of grief and loss and my heart is heavy with sorrow. I ask for your presence to be with me as I go through these most difficult days. Help me to find strength and comfort in you.

In my tears, I find refuge in you, knowing that your love endures forever. I trust in your promise of comfort and healing. Wrap your loving arms around me and protect me, I pray.

Give me the faith to know that, even in the darkest of nights, your light is shining and the morning of rejoicing will come. As I weep, I find reassurance in your eternal favour, which is a source of hope and renewal.

I ask for the wisdom to cherish the memories of my loved one and to hold onto the love we shared. Grant me the courage to face each day trusting in your plan and with hope for the future.

During this time of grief, help me to seek your presence and guidance, for I know that you are near to the broken-hearted. You are my rock and my refuge and in you, I find strength and comfort.

In Jesus' precious name, I pray. Amen.

Daily Journal

In his presence, my resting place

I have fought the good fight; I have finished the race.
In God's love, I have found my resting place.

The battles I faced, the storms I braved.
Through it all, my Jesus saved.

Through trials and tribulations, He held me near.
In moments of doubt and in times of fear.

The journey was challenging. The road was long.
But in his love, I always knew where I belonged.

Now, in his eternal kingdom, I've found my space.
In his infinite love, I've found my resting place.

The battles are over, the storms have ceased.
In his presence, I've found endless peace.

Find your comfort knowing that I rest,
In the arms of Jesus, eternally blessed.

In his love and grace, I've found my space.
And there in his presence, I've found my resting place.

Verse

2 Timothy 4:7: "I have fought the good fight, I have finished the race, I have kept the faith."

In this verse, Paul reflects on his life and ministry, expressing his readiness to face the end of his earthly journey.

Paul has faced challenges and struggles in his life and ministry. It signifies his commitment to living according to his faith, even when confronted with adversity. It encourages us to remain steadfast in our faith and to stand up for what is right, even in the face of difficulties.

Paul acknowledges that his life's journey and mission have come to a conclusion. He has fulfilled his purpose and completed the work he was called to do. This part of the verse reminds us that life is a journey with a beginning and an end and it encourages us to live with purpose and dedication. Paul affirms his unwavering commitment to his faith and his trust in God. Throughout his life, he has remained faithful to his beliefs and convictions. This part of the verse encourages us to hold onto our faith, even in the face of challenges and uncertainties.

Word of encouragement:

Let's find our inspiration and solace in the words of 2 Timothy 4:7, where Paul proclaimed, "I have fought the good fight, I have finished the race, I have kept the faith."

Today we can think of our loved ones and treasure the memories of a life well-lived, one marked by faith, courage and unwavering commitment to what is right.

Their journey on this earth may have reached its conclusion, but the legacy they leave behind is a testament to the goodness and grace of our Heavenly Father.

As we grieve the physical absence, let us also celebrate their remarkable journey.

They fought the good fight, embodying integrity, compassion and love. They finished the race, with dedication and purpose. And most importantly, they kept the faith, placing their trust in the loving arms of our heavenly Father.

In the presence of God, they found eternal peace, and their legacy of faith and goodness lives on in our hearts.

Let us honour their memory by carrying forward the values and virtues they held dear. May we too, continue to fight the good fight, finish the race of life with purpose and keep the faith, knowing that our Heavenly Father is our eternal refuge.

In our moments of sorrow, let us find comfort in the knowledge that they now rest with our Heavenly Father, where all tears are wiped away and pain is no more.

Prayer

Our Dear Heavenly Father, today I come before you seeking comfort and peace. I am reminded of the words of the apostle Paul in 2 Timothy 4:7, where he declared, "I have fought the good fight, I have finished the race, I have kept the faith." In this moment of sorrow, I find inspiration and encouragement in these words.

Father, may I find comfort in the memory of a life well-lived, marked by faith, courage, and an unwavering commitment to what is right. I know that, even though my loved one's earthly journey may have come to an end, their legacy of goodness and grace continues to shine brightly.

As I grieve their physical absence, I celebrate their remarkable journey. They fought the good fight, embodying integrity, compassion, and love. They finished the race with dedication and purpose. Most importantly, they kept the faith, trusting in you.

In your presence, I find eternal peace, and their legacy of faith and goodness lives on in my heart. I honour their memory by carrying forward the values and virtues they held dear.

I also pray for all those who mourn today, asking for your comfort and strength to envelop them. May they continue to fight the good fight, finish the race of life with purpose and keep the faith, knowing that you are their eternal refuge.

In my moments of sorrow, may I find solace in the knowledge that my loved ones now rest with you, where all tears are wiped away, and all pain is no more. I trust in your promise of eternal life and hold fast to my faith.

In Jesus' precious name, I pray. Amen.

Daily Journal

I smiled today

I smiled today,
Remembering the past,
The laughter we shared,
The games we played.
Those memories will forever last.

I smiled today
as I thought of the times we fought,
In conflicts and disagreements,
So many lessons were taught.

In our shared journey,
Through thick and thin,
I smiled today,
Remembering all that we have been through.

I smiled today,
recalling moments when we'd confide,
thinking of us, whispering secrets,
side by side.

I smiled today,
As I reflected upon the past.
The challenges, the victories.
What a blast.

Through these tears,
I find a way to smile.
For the time we had together,
I am so grateful,
Even if it was only for a little while.

I smiled today because of you.
For in every way,
I will always cherish you.

Verse

Ecclesiastes 3:4: "A time to weep and a time to laugh, a time to mourn and a time to dance."

This verse captures the essence of life's seasons, including moments of grief and mourning, as well as times of joy and celebration. It reminds us that life is marked by a natural ebb and flow of experiences and it's okay to go through different emotions, including weeping and mourning.

This verse encourages us to embrace each season of life, acknowledging that both moments of grief and moments of happiness are valuable and meaningful. It also offers us comfort as we go through difficult times, as it assures us that in due course, there will be a time to experience joy and celebrate life once again.

Word of encouragement:

In the journey of grief, Ecclesiastes 3:4 offers a message of hope and comfort. It reassures us that it's perfectly normal to grieve and mourn when we've lost a loved one. It acknowledges the tears and sorrow we experience during these times.

However, it also reminds us that, just as there are seasons of mourning, there will come a time for joy and celebration again. The pain we feel is a part of the healing process, and it doesn't last forever. It's essential to allow yourself to grieve and mourn, but also to be open to the moments of laughter and dancing that will eventually come.

In your grief, remember that it's a journey with different seasons. Your loved one's memory will bring both tears and smiles. Embrace each season as it comes, knowing that healing and joy are part of the natural order of life. You are not alone in your sorrow, and there is hope for brighter days ahead. Allow yourself the grace to grieve and the freedom to find joy once more.

Prayer

Our Dear Heavenly Father, today, I come before you for comfort and strength, guided by the wisdom of Ecclesiastes 3:4. Lord, help me to seek comfort in the understanding that life is marked by various experiences and emotions, including moments of both mourning and dancing.

Father, help me in my sorrow to know that weeping and mourning are natural and necessary responses to grief. Grant me the grace to grieve, to shed tears, and to remember my loved one with love and fondness.

Lord, your word says that there will be a time for laughter and dancing once again. May I find comfort in the assurance that joy will return. Grant me the strength to look ahead to the days when I can celebrate life once more.

Father, may I feel your presence, even in my tears and may you provide me with the courage to face each season of life. Lord, I know that I am not alone and that, in your time, healing and joy will come.

In my journey through grief, may I find moments of light amidst the darkness. I ask for your loving care to surround me. I know that you are the God of all seasons.

In Jesus' precious name, I pray. Amen.

Daily Journal

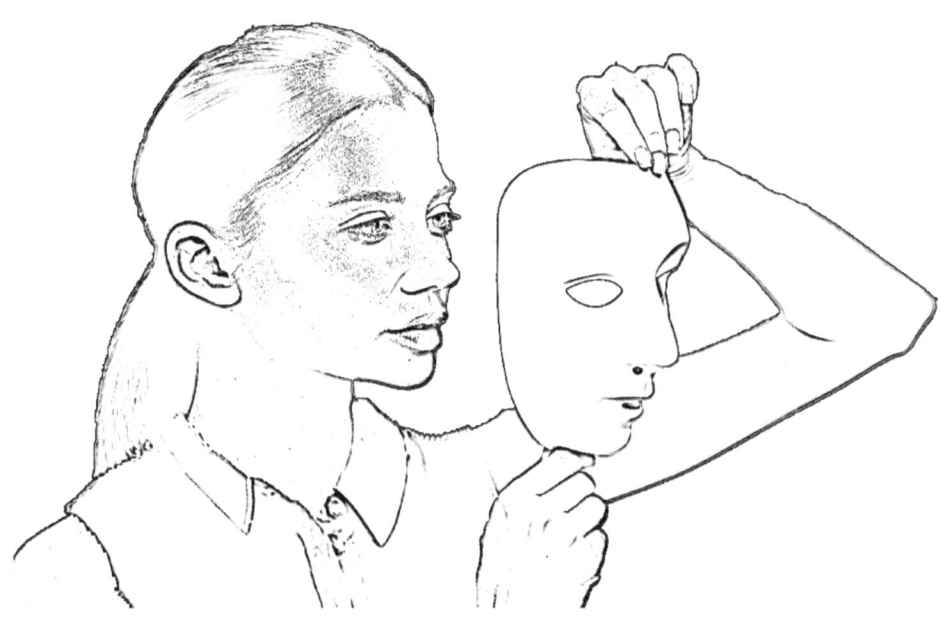

Removing the mask

Removing the mask, I'll embrace the day.
Dealing with grief, I'll find my way.

With each new sunrise, I see a brand-new start.
Here's another chance to mend the pieces of my heart.

The mask I wear, the tears I hide,
Always a silent battle deep inside.

The world may see a cheerful face,
But in my heart, there's an empty space.

The mask it's heavy, hard to bear,
This weight I carry everywhere.

But underneath, I'm not alone,
For others wear masks of their own.

The strength to heal begins within.
To heal, to mend, let the journey begin.

So, I thank you, Jesus, for your love and care,
For being with me through my despair.

Removing the mask, I'll heal through my grief.
Thank you, Lord, for being my relief.

Verse

Psalm 147:3: "He heals the broken-hearted and binds up their wounds."

This verse reassures us that, even in times of profound grief and brokenness, we are not alone. God is near, ready to heal the wounded heart and provide the comfort required to move forward. It is a reminder that healing is possible and that with God's help, we can find restoration and renewal, even in the most challenging of times. This verse reflects God's compassionate and loving nature as the ultimate healer of our broken hearts.

Word of encouragement:

Grief can feel overwhelming but there is hope in the promise of healing and restoration. God's love and compassion are a source of strength and he is ready to offer you comfort and solace during this challenging time.

As you navigate your journey through grief, remember that healing is possible. It may take time and the path may not always be straightforward, but God is there to guide you and provide the care and tenderness needed to bind up your wounds. Lean on his love and find refuge in his presence, for he is the ultimate healer of our broken hearts.

In your moments of sorrow, hold onto the promise of this verse, knowing that the pain you feel is not the end of your story. With God's help, you can find restoration and renewal and your heavy heart will gradually find relief.

Prayer

Our Dear Heavenly Father, today I am reminded of your promise to heal the broken-hearted and bind up their wounds.

Thank you for your compassion and love. I pray for the strength to remove the mask I've worn and begin the journey toward healing. Lord, I ask for your guidance and comfort as I navigate this path of grief. Help me find the inner strength to heal and mend my wounded heart. I trust in your unwavering love to carry me through this challenging time.

May I remember that I am not alone in my grief, for others also wear masks of their own. Give me the empathy to support those who walk similar journeys.

I pray for the restoration and renewal promised in your Word. Let your healing touch bind up my wounds and bring comfort to my soul. Lord, grant me the courage to face each day and embrace the healing power of your love.

Thank you, Lord, for being my relief in these difficult moments.

In Jesus' precious name, I pray. Amen.

Daily Journal

The language of tears

In times of loss and pain,
When words won't come,
My Jesus sees my tears,
Each, one by one.

In every heartfelt cry,
He guides my way.
For he understands
the language of tears, any day.

In the silence of my grief,
He can hear my heart cry.
And in those healing tears,
He is always close by.

Though I may stumble,
Unable to pray,
He understands the language of tears,
Night and day.

He knows the depth of my pain,
The burdens I bear.
And through my tears,
I know his presence is there.

In the language of tears,
He comprehends my heart.
In the silence of my struggle,
He plays the best part.

He's the author of my story,
Wiping away my tears.
The one that holds me dear,
Calming all my fears.

With every tear that falls,
A new chapter starts,
For in the story of my tears,
He will always heal my broken heart.

Verse

Psalm 56:8: "You keep track of all my sorrows. You have collected all my tears in your bottle. You have recorded each one in your book."

This verse signifies that God is intimately aware of our sorrows, collects our tears as a sign of his compassion and keeps a record of our emotional experiences. This verse offers us comfort, assuring us that God is intimately involved in our lives and empathises with our pain and distress.

Word of encouragement:

During this challenging time, it's normal to feel overwhelmed by your sorrows and tears. But please take heart in the knowledge that God is not distant or indifferent to your suffering. He is intimately aware of every sorrow you carry and he cherishes each tear you shed as a symbol of his deep compassion.

God doesn't forget your pain or your struggles; he keeps a record of them in his book. You are not alone in your grief, for He is with you, taking note of every emotional experience you go through.

As you navigate your journey through grief, remember that God's love and understanding are unwavering. Your tears are precious to him and your sorrows are not in vain. You are seen and known by the one who cares for you deeply.

May you find comfort in God's presence, knowing that He is a God of empathy and solace. In your moments of sorrow, lean on him and allow him to collect your tears and record your pain in his book of love. Your journey through grief is not one you walk alone; God is your constant companion, ready to provide the comfort and support you need.

Prayer

Dear Lord Jesus, in my time of sorrow and grief, I find comfort in your presence and the words of Psalm 56:8. I know, Lord, that you are aware of my sorrows and you collect every tear I shed as a sign of your deep compassion. I take comfort in knowing that you will never forget my pain or struggles.

Through my mourning and heartache, I know that I am not alone in my grief, for you are with me, taking note of every emotional experience I go through.

Thank you, Lord, for your love and understanding that is unwavering. I believe that my tears are precious to you, and my sorrow is not in vain. I know that you love me beyond measure.

May I find peace in your presence. In my moments of sorrow, I lean on you and trust you to collect my tears and record my pain in your book of love. Thank you that I am not on this journey through grief alone; you are my constant companion, ready to provide the comfort and support I need.

Grant me the strength to navigate this season of mourning, the courage to face my sorrows, and the assurance that in your love, I will find refuge.

In Jesus' precious name, I pray. Amen.

Daily Journal

My mirror

My mirror has seen it all.
The highs and lows, the rise and fall.
But Jesus sees the real me,
And that's who I long to be.

My mirror watches me laugh, watches me cry.
Through every storm that passes me by.
Yet in the mirror's gaze, I remember the key,
Jesus looks past the surface, He only sees the real me.

In the mirror's gaze, I find my reflection.
A face that carries both pain and affection.
But in His eyes, I am cherished for eternity.
He sees the real me, and that's where I want to be.

In the mirror, my story is in every line.
The laughter, the tears, recalling the moments of time.
Yet in his compassionate gaze, it's easy to see.
He sees the real me, and his love sets me free.

In that reflective glass, the pain looks so real.
With all the sorrow and grief, the hurt that I feel.
I turn to Jesus, his love I can feel,
With him by my side, my heart begins to heal.

Today, in front of that reflective glass, I kneel.
In his loving embrace all my pain he conceals.

I know that with his grace and compassion,
My wounds will seal. In His presence, I will truly heal.

Verse

Psalm 139:1-4: "1 You have searched me, Lord, and you know me. 2 You know when I sit and when I rise; you perceive my thoughts from afar. 3 You discern my going out and my lying down; you are familiar with all my ways. 4 Before a word is on my tongue you, Lord, know it completely."

This passage highlights the depth of God's knowledge and understanding of us. It tells us that God knows our innermost thoughts, actions and the intricacies of our lives. He perceives us on a level that goes beyond what any mirror or human understanding can provide. God sees and loves us for who we truly are, beyond our outward appearance and life's ups and downs.

Word of encouragement:

In your moments of mourning and grief, let these beautiful words and the profound Scripture from Psalm 139:1-4 bring you comfort and encouragement.

Your reflection in the mirror may reveal the highs and lows, the laughter, and the tears, but always remember that God sees you on a much deeper level. He knows you intimately, even the thoughts you haven't spoken aloud. He understands the pain and sorrow that may not be immediately visible.

In your journey through grief, take solace in the fact that God's love and compassion extend beyond the surface. He cherishes you for who you truly are and His grace is there to heal your wounds. You are not alone in this process.

As you kneel before him, know that His presence is your source of healing and through his grace, you will find the strength to heal and move forward. Your true self, cherished and loved by God, is the path to recovery and renewal.

May you find peace and comfort in the knowledge that God knows you completely and loves you deeply. Your journey through grief may be challenging, but you are never alone in it. The real you, seen and cherished by your Creator, is where you'll find solace, healing, and hope.

You are not alone and God's love is a constant presence offering you strength and comfort.

Prayer

Dear Heavenly Father, as I gather in your presence, I am comforted by the truth in Psalm 139:1-4. You know me intimately, you know my every action, my thoughts and my ways.

In this moment of mourning and grief, I find comfort in the knowledge that you see and understand me in a way no one else can.

I am thankful that your love is boundless, and you cherish me for who I truly am.

Lord, through this season of grieving and mourning, be my refuge and strength. Comfort me with the reassurance that you know my deepest pain and my most profound joys. Lord, be with me every step of the way.

Help me to find healing and strength in knowing that you see and love me for my true self.

Lord, I trust in your unfailing love and understanding, even when my heart is heavy with grief. Thank you for being my constant source of comfort and for seeing me beyond my imperfections.

In Jesus' precious name, I pray. Amen.

Daily Journal

A piece of me ...

Chase your dreams,
Don't delay or hold back.
In your accomplishments, your success,
Stay on track.

With every milestone reached,
Every goal achieved, you'll always carry a piece of me.

I am watching over you from a heavenly place,
Every ambition and every goal you chase.
Pursue your dreams at your own pace,
But kneel in prayer to find the strength
to move forward with grace.

In your journey ahead, on bended knees,
You can achieve all your dreams.
Reach for the stars, cross over the seas.
With faith as your compass,
You can do whatever you please.

Though doubt may try to deter you, stand tall.
In the face of challenges, rise above them all.
On bended knees, you'll find the strength,
And the courage to go to any length.
So, chase your dreams, don't delay or hold back,
In your accomplishments, in your success,
Stay on track.

With every milestone reached,
Every goal achieved; you'll always carry a piece of me.

So, remember this truth as you journey along,
Your potential is boundless –
In your accomplishments, your success,
On bended knees, you can achieve your dreams.
And there my legacy will always be.

Verse

Philippians 4:13: "I can do all things through Christ who strengthens me."

The verse tells us that through a relationship with Christ, we can find the strength to face and overcome various challenges and circumstances in life.

We can overcome obstacles, achieve goals, and endure hardships with Christ's help.

Our own strength may be limited, but with Christ's strength, we can accomplish more than we could on our own.

It reminds us that we are not alone in our struggles and that we can find the strength to persevere and achieve our goals through our relationship with Him.

Word of encouragement:

During your grief and mourning, I want to remind you of a powerful truth encapsulated in Philippians 4:13: "I can do all things through Christ who strengthens me." Even during the most challenging times, you are not alone in your journey and you possess an incredible wellspring of strength.

You have the capacity to achieve your dreams. Through faith and prayer, you can find the strength to move forward with grace and resilience. On bended knees, you can overcome hurdles and achieve remarkable things.

Remember that the grief and mourning you are experiencing may try to deter you, but with your faith as your compass, you can rise above challenges and reach for the stars. You have the strength to stand tall and keep moving forward, even when doubt attempts to hold you back.

The verse from Philippians speaks of the limitless strength that comes through your relationship with Christ. Lean on this strength during your mourning and use it as a source of inspiration and courage. With Christ's help, you can overcome, endure, and achieve.

In the memory of your loved one and the legacy they've left, they would want to see you thrive, chase your dreams, and find success. So, pursue your ambitions and goals with the knowledge that their love and influence remain with you, and Christ's strength will empower you to achieve incredible things.

Stay strong, keep the faith. Your journey continues and your loved one's legacy lives on through you.

Prayer

Dear Lord Jesus, you understand the weight of my sorrow and the depth of my pain. You know the struggles I face, and I find comfort in the knowledge that I am not alone. I know that, through my faith and relationship with Christ, I can find the resilience and strength to endure and eventually heal.

During this difficult journey, I lean on you, dear Lord. Please grant me the strength to carry on and the courage to face the obstacles that lie ahead. When the pain feels overwhelming, remind me that I can do all things through Christ who strengthens me.

As I walk this path of grief and mourning, I also remember my loved one, who is now with you in a heavenly place. I know they would want me to pursue my dreams and fulfill my potential.

May your comforting presence surround me, Lord, and may your love sustain me during this time of mourning. Help me find the strength to endure, heal and eventually experience moments of peace and joy once more. I place my trust in you, for you are my refuge and my source of strength.

In Jesus' precious name, I pray. Amen.

Daily Journal

A promise I'll keep...

In the depths of sorrow,
when hearts are torn,
I find solace in God's promise.
To heal other hearts that mourn.

In your memory,
I'll offer strength and grace,
A promise I'll keep
to care for those in the same sorrowful space.

When someone feels all alone and abandoned,
I'll share my father's love so they're not stranded.
I'll remind them of a promise from above,
"The Lord is close to the broken-hearted,"
with boundless love.

In moments of grief, when words are few,
A promise I'll keep, it's my presence that will speak.

Through the pain I know, the tears I weep,
A promise I'll keep is understanding how others feel.

As I honour your memory,
The promise is clear.
That with each act of kindness, you are near.

You left a legacy of kindness,
compassion, generosity and grace.
This is a promise I'll keep,
to care for those who grieve and weep.

Verse

2 Corinthians 1:3-4: "Praise be to the God and Father of our Lord Jesus Christ, the Father of compassion and the God of all comfort, who comforts us in all our troubles, so that we can comfort those in any trouble with the comfort we ourselves receive from God."

This verse teaches us that God is the Father of compassion and the God of all comfort.

In times of trouble, God provides comfort and solace to those who turn to him. Furthermore, the verse highlights that the comfort we receive from God is not meant to be selfishly hoarded. Instead, it is intended to be shared with others who are also in need of comfort.

In receiving God's comfort, we are then equipped to offer comfort to others who are going through similar troubles.

The verse reflects the idea that God's comfort is not just for our benefit but also for us to be channels of his compassion and comfort to those around us who are facing difficulties and hardships.

Word of encouragement:

In your moments of sorrow, take heart in the knowledge that you are not alone. God is there, ready to wrap you in his comforting embrace. He is the God of all comfort and his compassion knows no bounds.

Furthermore, this verse encourages us to share the comfort we receive from God with others who are also in need. As you go through your journey of grief and mourning, remember that your own experiences of God's comfort can become a source of strength for someone else. Your empathy and compassion can be a guiding light for those who are struggling.

You are not just a recipient of God's comfort, you are a vessel through which his comfort flows to touch the lives of others.

As you find healing and peace in your own mourning, extend a hand of support to those around you who are also in need.

Remember that, even in the midst of sorrow, there is a profound sense of purpose and an opportunity to be an instrument of God's comfort to others.

Your experiences can make a meaningful difference in the lives of those who share in your journey of grief.

May you find strength and comfort in God's boundless compassion and may your journey through mourning become a source of hope and healing for others as well.

Prayer

Dear Lord Jesus, today I thank you for being a compassionate Father and for being in my life.

As I navigate this difficult path of mourning, I take comfort in the knowledge that you understand my troubles and pain.

Lord, help me to carry the lessons I learn from my grief and my journey toward healing, as a source of comfort to others who may also be facing those same troubles and hardships. Make me a vessel of your compassion, ready to extend a hand of support and empathy to those in need.

May my mourning not be in vain but serve as a beacon of hope and healing for others who cross my path. I ask for your strength and guidance as I navigate this journey and I pray for the wisdom and compassion to be a source of comfort to those around me.

In your everlasting love and boundless compassion, I find comfort. As you lead me through this season of mourning, enable me to channel your comfort to those who need it.

In Jesus' precious name, I pray. Amen.

Daily Journal

In the stillness of 2am

In the stillness of 2 am, I lie awake,
There, in the dark, my heart begins to ache.

A silent room, the world's asleep,
As I lie here thinking, my thoughts run deep.

Memories of you flood my mind,
In the quiet night, comfort is hard to find.

I toss and turn, searching for sleep,
But in the darkness, my tears run deep.

In the quiet night, my heart's heavy and worn,
I turn to God's grace in the stillness of this morn.

The burdens I carry, in his hands I lay,
I know His comforting grace will lead me to a brighter day.

With each whispered prayer, my heart freely poured
When I speak to my Lord, my hope is restored.

The darkness recedes, and the burden grows light,
In the quiet of dawn, everything feels just right.

In the stillness of 2 am, prayer is the key,
In those precious hours, His light and love sets me free.

Verse

Matthew 11:28: "Come to me, all you who are weary and burdened, and I will give you rest."

In this verse, Jesus is addressing those who are feeling tired, burdened, or spiritually weary. It's an invitation to people who are struggling with the challenges and hardships of life. Jesus is offering them solace, relief, and a sense of rest, not only in a physical sense but also in a spiritual and emotional sense.

If you come to Jesus and place your burdens on him, you can find a type of rest that goes beyond physical relaxation. It's a promise of finding peace, comfort and spiritual renewal during life's difficulties.

This verse has been a source of comfort and encouragement for many people facing life's trials, offering the assurance that they can turn to their faith and find rest and solace in times of trouble.

Word of Encouragement:

In the darkest hours of the night, when you lie awake with a heavy heart and the memories of your loved one flood your thoughts, turn to the Lord.

Your pain and sorrow are not carried alone. Just as you lay your burdens in God's hands, remember that he offers rest for the weary and comfort for the burdened.

Grief can be a long and difficult journey, but in the stillness of the night, through whispered prayers and your heartfelt conversations with the Lord, you can find hope and solace.

Your tears and heartache do not go unnoticed by your Creator and in his grace, you will discover the strength to face a new day.

As you carry the burdens of your loss, know that the Lord's love and light can set you free from the darkness that surrounds you.

Your hope will be restored, and even in the stillness of 2 am, you can find moments of comfort and grace.

May God's presence be your guiding light as you navigate through this season of mourning and grieving. Lean on your faith and the comforting grace of the Lord, for in his love you will find the strength to carry on.

Prayer

Our Dear Heavenly Father, when the weight of grief and sorrow feels almost unbearable, I turn to you, my refuge and my strength.

Lord, you know the depths of my pain and the heaviness in my heart and I seek your comfort and guidance during this season of mourning and grieving.

I thank you for the promise you've given me in Matthew 11:28, where you invite me to come to you when I am weary and burdened, assuring me that you will provide rest. In these moments of solitude and darkness, I find solace in your loving arms.

Lord, I lay before you the memories of my loved one that flood my mind in the quiet of the night. I acknowledge that comfort can be hard to find during these times, but I trust in your grace. I surrender the burdens I carry into your hands, knowing that your comforting grace will lead me to brighter days. In these precious hours, in whispered prayers, my hope is restored.

In the quiet of dawn, everything feels just right as your love and light set me free. I pray for strength and guidance as I navigate this difficult journey of grief.

May your presence be my guiding light, leading me toward healing and solace. I trust in your promise to provide rest and comfort for the weary and burdened.

In Jesus' precious name, I pray. Amen.

Daily Journal

Lonely, but not alone

I feel alone in this time you are gone,
The silence around me, the ache lingers on.

The world moves forward, yet I stand still.
With an emptiness, an absence, I struggle to fill.

People stay away, they don't know what to say.
I feel alone in this moment's grey.

The silence surrounds me, my heart's heavy with sorrow,
Why is everyone distant? Will it be the same tomorrow?

Though the world may change and people may part.
In the arms of my Savior, I'll find a brand-new start.

Though the world may turn its back and friends may fade.
In his love and light, my path is truly paved.

Lonely, but not alone, Jesus is always near.
In his presence, I'll find comfort and cheer.

In the quiet moments, he is always by my side.
In his boundless love, he always provides.

Lonely, but not alone, by his grace and guidance,
I find my guiding light, and in his loving presence …
everything feels just right.

Verse

Matthew 28:20: "And surely I am with you always, to the very end of the age."

In this verse, Jesus is assuring his disciples and all believers of His continued presence and support. He is promising to be with us always, without exception, until the end of the age.

This means that no matter the circumstances, challenges, or changes the world may undergo, Jesus' presence and guidance will remain constant. It offers solace, comfort and a sense of security.

Even when facing adversity, uncertainties, or difficult times, we can draw strength from the knowledge that Jesus is with us, offering support, guidance and spiritual companionship.

Word of Encouragement:

It's entirely natural to feel alone and isolated during these times, to see the world move forward while your heart aches with sorrow. The silence that surrounds you can be overwhelming and the distance from others can be hard to bear. But remember, you are not alone.

You are never alone in your journey, for Jesus is always with you. His presence is a constant source of comfort, a beacon of light in the darkest moments. His love never departs and it shines brightly even when the world may seem distant.

Take each day one step at a time and allow his love to surround and uplift you. Your path is paved with his unwavering support and his presence will bring you the comfort and cheer you need to find healing and solace.

May you find strength in your faith and the enduring love of Jesus as you journey through this season of mourning and grief.

Prayer

Our Dear Heavenly Father, I come before you in prayer to seek comfort and upliftment during this season of mourning and grieving.

Lord, I come before you with a heavy heart, feeling the loneliness that accompanies the absence of my dear loved one.

I hold firm to the promise from Matthew 28:20, where you assure me that you are with me always, to the very end of the age.

Lord Jesus, as the world continues to move forward, I may feel as if I am standing still, struggling to fill the emptiness left by the departure of my loved one.

Friends and family may stay away, not knowing the right words to say, leaving me to wonder why I feel so isolated. But I know, Lord, that your presence is ever near.

In the stillness of these moments, I find solace in your love and I recognise that even when the world seems distant, you are always present.

Heavenly Father, I pray that you uplift me during this season of mourning and grieving. Help me find strength, healing and the peace that surpasses all understanding.

May your boundless love be my guiding light, illuminating the path toward restoration and hope.

In Jesus' precious name, I pray. Amen.

Daily Journal

Beyond the Door

In the stillness of my room, I stand alone,
A heart heavy with sorrow, in my own zone.

The world outside calls, a life to explore,
But explaining your absence is a heavy chore.

For beyond the door, there's a life to explore,
But I fear the questions, the ones I can't ignore.

The people I'll encounter, the friends I'll meet,
Will ask about your absence and my heart skips a beat.

I know that beyond the door, there's a life to explore,
Though I'm scared of the words, of the tears that may pour.

The thought of explaining, reliving the pain,
Seems like a burden, an unending chain.

But with the strength of the Lord, I will regain
the courage to venture beyond – where healing reigns.

So, I will trust in the Lord as I go beyond the door,
In his comforting presence, my heart will be restored.

Verse

Isaiah 41:10: "So do not fear, for I am with you; do not be dismayed, for I am your God. I will strengthen you and help you; I will uphold you with my righteous right hand."

This verse is a source of great comfort and encouragement for us who face fear, uncertainty, or adversity. It reminds us of God's presence, his willingness to strengthen and support us and his promise to uphold us with his righteous hand. It reflects a message of faith, trust and reliance on God's protection and care in challenging times.

Word of Encouragement:

In times of sorrow and grief, when standing alone with a heavy heart, it's natural to feel hesitant about venturing beyond the door.

But remember the powerful verse from Isaiah 41:10, which offers a comforting message: "So do not fear, for I am with you; do not be dismayed, for I am your God. I will strengthen you and help you, I will uphold you with my righteous right hand."

God's presence and his unwavering support are with you, especially during these challenging moments. It's completely understandable to have fears and burdens but have faith that he will provide you with the strength and courage you need to heal.

You are not alone on this journey and the Lord's comforting presence will help your heart restore. As you continue to navigate beyond the door, may you find the healing you seek and may the love of the Lord surround you with peace and restoration.

Prayer

Our Dear Heavenly Father, today I come before knowing that in my time of sorrow and grief, you are our rock and refuge. I thank you for the reassurance of Isaiah 41:10: "So do not fear, for I am with you; do not be dismayed, for I am your God. I will strengthen you and help you; I will uphold you with my righteous right hand."

Lord, as I venture beyond the door into a world that has changed in the absence of my loved one, I carry the burden of explaining the pain I bear.

But today, I trust in your strength, Lord. I believe that you will grant me the courage to face the questions, to speak the words, and to heal from the pain. I know that you are with me, upholding me with your righteous right hand.

In this season of mourning and grieving, I pray for your presence to surround me. Be my comfort, my strength and my guide. Help me to find healing and restoration as I trust in you. May your love bring peace to my heavy heart.

In Jesus' precious name, I pray, Amen.

Daily Journal

Shadows in our home

There is something I must say,
Our home has changed since the day you went away.
Shadows in our home, as we face each day.
Your presence once so bright now seems so far away.

The spaces you once filled now stand as silent proof,
Of all the joy and love you brought beneath this roof.
The rooms feel empty with you not in sight,
But the memories you left, still shine bright.

Your laughter, your smile, still linger in the air,
A testament to the love we were so lucky to share.
Though you're no longer with us in body, it's true,
In our faith and our love, we will keep feeling you.

Your laughter echoes still in the stories we share,
In our memories, in our hearts, we know you're always there.
Though shadows may surround us, with Jesus, we won't fall,
With his everlasting love, we will conquer it all.

Verse

1 Thessalonians 4:13-14: "Brothers and sisters, we do not want you to be uninformed about those who sleep in death so that you do not grieve like the rest of mankind, who have no hope. For we believe that Jesus died and rose again, and so we believe that God will bring with Jesus those who have fallen asleep in him."

This verse emphasises that we should not grieve without hope when our loved ones die. Our hope must be based on the death and resurrection of Jesus Christ. The passage assures that when Jesus returns, he will bring with him those who have died, emphasising the hope of resurrection and reunion for all faithful followers. It is a message of comfort and assurance in the face of death, highlighting the unique hope that we can have in the resurrection.

Word of Encouragement

As you navigate through the shadows of loss and sorrow, remember that your loved one's memory lives on in the stories you share, the laughter you remember and the love that still resides in your heart. The pain of their absence may be sharp, but the enduring hope we find in the promise of resurrection, as mentioned in 1 Thessalonians 4:13-14, reminds us that separation is not the end.

In the midst of your grief, you are not alone. In your faith and love, your loved one's spirit lives on and you can continue to feel their presence, even if it's not in the same way as before. Your loved one's laughter echoes in the stories you share and their love remains in your heart.

Though shadows may surround you, take solace in the belief that with Jesus and his everlasting love, you can conquer even the deepest grief. Lean on the faith and hope provided by the Bible verse from 1 Thessalonians 4:13-14, knowing that the promise of reunion and resurrection offers solace in the face of loss.

May you find strength, peace and the healing power of love as you mourn and cherish the beautiful memories of your loved one.

Prayer

Dear Lord Jesus, today I find solace in the words of 1 Thessalonians 4:13-14, which remind me not to grieve without hope.

I know that my loved one's spirit lives on in your presence and I take comfort in the promise of resurrection and reunion through your grace.

Lord, I offer this prayer for myself and all those who are mourning the loss of someone dear to them. We come together, seeking your presence and strength during this difficult time.

Today, I remember my loved one and the light they brought into my life. I am grateful for the memories we hold and all the stories we shared.

Lord, grant me the peace that surpasses all understanding. Help me to conquer the shadows of grief with the hope and promise of resurrection.

Be my refuge and strength as I mourn and grieve. I ask for your healing touch to heal my broken heart and your light to guide me through the darkest hours. May your love be a constant source of comfort and strength.

In Jesus' precious name, I pray. Amen.

Daily Journal

Why me?

Sorry, Lord, if I ever asked, "Why me?"
Sorry for my moments of despair,
I doubted your plans, life just felt so unfair.

Sorry, Lord, if I ever asked, "Why me?"
In those moments of sorrow, I couldn't see.
Sorry, Lord, if I ever asked, "Why me?"
It just felt like you were punishing me.

Sorry, Lord, in my anger and doubt,
I questioned your ways, my faith timed out.
Forgive me, Lord, for doubting your plans,
In my moments of weakness, I failed to understand.

Forgive me, Lord, for the blame and the cries,
In those moments of sorrow,
my faith was compromised.

Forgive me, Lord, for doubting your plans,
In my moments of weakness, I failed to understand.
Thank you, Lord, for your forgiveness and grace,
now in your love, I forever will stand.

Verse

1 John 1:9: "If we confess our sins, he is faithful and just and will forgive us our sins and purify us from all unrighteousness."

This verse emphasises the importance of confessing our sins to God. When we do so, God, in his faithfulness and justice, forgives our sins and purifies us from unrighteousness, reconciling us with him and granting us a fresh start in our relationship with him. It highlights the grace and mercy of God available to those who humble themselves and seek his forgiveness.

Word of Encouragement:

During times of grief, it's perfectly natural to question, to feel angry and to wonder why certain things happen. Our willingness to express these feelings and seek forgiveness from the Lord shows our deep and honest connection with him.

The verse from 1 John 1:9 reminds us that when we confess our sins and turn to God with an open heart, he is faithful and just to forgive us and cleanse us from all unrighteousness. This promise serves as a source of hope and comfort during this challenging period.

As you move through this mourning and grieving process, please remember that your emotions are valid. The Lord understands your heart and your struggles. He is there to offer comfort, strength, and forgiveness.

Remember that your faith is your guiding light. Your faith in God's grace, forgiveness, and the promise of eternity can provide you with the hope and strength needed to navigate this period of grief.

Prayer

Our Dear Heavenly Father, I am so grateful for your unwavering love and understanding.

I am sorry, Lord, for the times I asked, "Why me?"; for the moments of despair when I questioned your plans and life felt so unfair.

I'm sorry for my moments of doubt, when my faith wavered and I couldn't see the way forward. In my anger and confusion, I questioned your ways, but today, I come before you with a humble heart seeking your forgiveness.

Your Word in 1 John 1:9 reminds me that when I confess my sins, you are faithful and just to forgive and purify me from all unrighteousness. I find comfort in your promise of forgiveness and cleansing, knowing that your grace is sufficient for me.

Lord, I don't have all the answers, but I find peace in knowing that one day we will be reunited in your presence. Thank you for your constant presence and unwavering love.

Wrap your loving arms around me as waves of grief threaten to overcome me. Be my refuge and stronghold, my strength in times of need.

Thank you for being a faithful friend who carries our sorrows, grief and pain. Help us to bring everything to you in prayer and to find comfort, peace and strength in your presence.

In Jesus' precious name, I pray. Amen.

Daily Journal

An everyday prayer for mourning and grieving

Lord, today I ask you to embrace me as my heart overflows with grief and unanswered questions. Jesus, you said, "Blessed are those who mourn, for they will be comforted" and today I ask you, Lord, to lift my eyes to you so that I can catch a glimpse of eternity and be comforted by the promise of heaven.

Give me hope in my confusion and grace to live by giving thanks to you. Let me cherish all the good memories, and give me the joy and peace through your Holy Spirit. Comfort my family, bind our hearts as one and help us to be united in our loss.

Lord, your word says you are close to the broken-hearted and those whose spirits are crushed. I ask you to draw close to me and rescue me from this pain and grief.

Help me to find strength and peace in your presence. Lord even as I am consumed with the pain and grief of this separation, I know that we will be reunited one day. Even in this sorrow I thank you for your promises.

Father, you promised that those who have hope in you will have their strength renewed. They will soar on wings like eagles. They will run and not grow weary. They will walk and not be faint. Give me the strength, Lord, as it is sometimes so hard to find rest in the midst of pain, worries and doubt. But I will stand on your word as it says 'even though I walk through the darkest valley, I will fear no evil, for you are with me, your rod and your staff, they comfort me'. Help me in this difficult time, that I can find my comfort, peace, and strength in you. Be with me every hour of every day, I need you, Lord.

Father, even as this pains me so much, and I don't have all the answers, and I struggle to understand, I will not question you. I find peace in knowing that to be absent from this body is to be at present with the Lord. And I thank you for this assurance that on that glorious day we will meet again.

Heavenly Father, I ask you to wrap your loving arms around me when waves of grief rise and threaten to overcome me. Father, I ask for your love and mercy to sustain me in my time of need. Be my refuge and stronghold as I go through this most difficult time. Watch over me as I sleep and help me each morning to face a new day.

I ask you to hear my prayers and comfort me as I deal with this unbearable loss. Help me to find strength and peace in your presence. What a faithful friend I have in you. You carry my sorrow, grief and my pain. Thank you, Lord, that I can bring everything to you in Prayer.

In Jesus' precious name, I pray, Amen.

Prayer for myself

Dear Heavenly Father, today I humbly come before you. I thank you, Lord, for the very breath of life. Today, I ask you to give me a spirit of humility when I deal with others. I pray that I will always be grateful for all that I have and to always remember that I have gained nothing on my own. As I humble myself before you, I ask, Lord, if anything is not of you let it be destroyed in Jesus' name.

Lord, your word says that you give wisdom to those who ask. Today, Father, I ask for your wisdom as I go about my day. Father, I cannot do anything without you; I ask for your love, guidance, and protection. Cover me under your mighty blood. Thank you, Lord, for loving me unconditionally. Thank you that when I am weak, you are strong. Help me not to lean on my own understanding but in everything acknowledge you so that you can direct my words, thoughts, and actions.

Thank you, Lord, that I am fearfully and wonderfully made. Help me learn how to face every storm with confidence. Father, today I lay my burdens at your feet. Forgive me if I have wronged anyone. Help me be slow to speak and slow to anger. Protect me from the pain of this world, Lord. I break every generational curse in Jesus' name.

Your word says that you have plans to prosper me and not to harm me, plans to give me hope and a future. Today I claim this Blessing in Jesus' name.

Lord Jesus, I know that I am a sinner. By faith I gratefully receive your gift of salvation. I am ready to trust you as my Lord and

Saviour. Thank you, Lord Jesus, for saving me. I believe you are the Son of God who died on the cross for my sins and rose from the dead on the third day. Thank you for bearing my sins and giving me the gift of eternal life. I believe your words are true. Come into my heart, Lord Jesus, and be my Saviour.

In Jesus' precious name, I pray. Amen.

Matthew 21:22 says, "If you believe, you will receive whatever you ask for in prayer."

Daily Journal

Daily Journal

Daily Journal

Daily Journal

Daily Journal

Daily Journal

Daily Journal

Daily Journal

About the Author

Pamela Govender is the compassionate author behind the book *I Smiled Today: A Book on Mourning and Healing*. Pamela has channelled her personal experiences into a remarkable collection of poems that offer solace, inspiration and guidance to those navigating the treacherous waters of mourning.

Her journey into the world of writing as a means of healing began with profound personal loss that shattered her world. During these trying times, she turned to the written word as a therapeutic outlet to make sense of her grief. Writing became an essential tool for Pamela, allowing her to confront her emotions head-on, express her deepest thoughts and slowly pave a path toward healing. Her words served as a lifeline, guiding her through the darkness and gradually leading her toward the light.

Within its pages, readers will find a message of hope, a source of strength and a beacon of light in the darkest of times. *I Smiled Today* serves as a reminder that, even in the midst of profound sorrow, there is the potential for healing, growth and the eventual return of joy.

www.ingramcontent.com/pod-product-compliance
Lightning Source LLC
Chambersburg PA
CBHW020143130526
44591CB00030B/181